teacher's friend publications

January

a creative idea book
for the
elementary teacher

written and illustrated
by
Karen Sevaly

Copyright © 1987
Teacher's Friend Publications, Inc.
All rights reserved
Printed in the United States of America
Published by Teacher's Friend Publications, Inc.
7407 Orangewood Drive, Riverside, CA 92504

ISBN-0-943263-04-2

TO TEACHERS AND CHILDREN EVERYWHERE.

Table of Contents

Making the Most of It!

WHAT IS IN
THIS BOOK:

You will find the following in each monthly idea book from Teacher's Friend Publications:

1. A calendar listing every day of the month with a classroom idea.

2. At least four new student awards to be sent home to parents.

3. Three new bookmarks that can be used in your school library or given to students by you as "Super Student Awards."

4. Numerous bulletin board ideas and patterns pertaining to the particular month.

5. Easy to make craft ideas related to the monthly holidays.

6. Dozens of activities emphasizing not only the obvious holidays but also chapters related to such subjects as; Eskimos and Chinese New Year.

7. Crossword puzzles, word finds, creative writing pages, booklet covers and much more.

8. Scores of classroom management techniques, the newest and the best.

HOW TO USE
THIS BOOK:

Every page of this book may be duplicated for individual classroom use.

Some pages are meant to be used as duplicating masters and used as student work sheets. Other pages may be copied onto construction paper or used as they are.

If you have access to a print shop, you will find that many pages work well when printed on index paper. This type of paper takes crayons and felt markers well and is sturdy enough to last and last. The wheel pattern and bookmarks are two items that work particularly well on index paper.

Lastly, some pages are meant to be enlarged with an overhead or opaque projector. When we say enlarge, we mean it! Think BIG! Three, four or even five feet is great! Try using colored butcher paper or poster board so you don't spend all your time coloring.

JANUARY

Making the Most of It!

ADDING THE
COLOR:

Putting the color to finished items can be a real bother to teachers in a rush. Try these ideas:

1. On small areas, water color markers work great. If your area is rather large switch to crayons or even colored chalk or pastels.

    (Don't worry, lamination or a spray fixative will keep the color on the work and off of you. No laminator or fixative? That's okay, a little hair spray will do the trick.)

2. The quickest method of coloring large items is to simply start with colored paper. (Poster board, butcher paper and large construction paper work well.) Add a few dashes of a contrasting colored marker or crayon and you will have it made.

3. Try cutting character eyes, teeth, etc. from white typing paper and gluing them in place. These features will really stand out and make your bulletin boards come alive.

    For special effects add real buttons or lace. Metallic paper looks great on stars and belt buckles, too.

LAMINATORS:

If you have access to a roll laminator you already know how fortunate you are. They are priceless when it comes to saving time and money. Try these ideas:

1. You can laminate more than just classroom posters and construction paper. Try various kinds of fabric, wall paper and gift wrapping. You'll be surprised at the great combinations you come up with.

    Laminated classified ads can be used to cut headings for current event bulletin boards. Colorful gingham fabric makes terrific cut letters or scalloped edging. You might even try burlap! It looks terrific on a fall bulletin board.

    (You can even make professional looking bookmarks with laminated fabric or burlap. They are great gift ideas.)

2. Felt markers and laminated paper or fabric can work as a team. Just make sure the markers you use are permanent and not water based. Oops, make a mistake! That's okay. Put a little ditto fluid on a tissue, rub across the mark and presto, it's gone! (Dry transfer markers work great on lamination, too.)

LAMINATORS:
(continued)

DITTO MASTERS:

3. Laminating cut-out characters can be tricky. If you have enlarged an illustration onto poster board, simply laminate first and then cut it out with an art knife. (Just make sure the laminator is plenty hot.)

One problem may arise when you paste an illustration onto poster board and laminate the finished product. If your paste-up does not cover 100% of the illustration, the poster board may separate from it after laminating. To avoid this problem, paste your illustration onto poster board that measures slightly larger. This way, the lamination will help hold down your illustration.

Have you ever laminated student-made place mats, crayon shavings, tissue paper collages, or dried flowers? You'll be amazed at the variety of creative things that can be laminated and used in the classroom, or as take-home gifts.

Many of the pages in this book can be made into masters for duplicating. Try some of these ideas for best results:

1. When using new masters, turn down the pressure on the duplicating machine. As the copies become light, increase the pressure. This will get longer wear out of both the master and the machine.

2. If the print from the back side of your original comes through the front when making a master or photocopy, slip a sheet of black construction paper behind the sheet. This will mask the unwanted black lines and create a much better copy.

3. Trying to squeeze one more run out of that worn master can be frustrating. Try lightly spraying the inked side of the master with hair spray. For some reason, this helps the master put out those few extra copies.

4. Several potential masters in this book contain instructions for the teacher. Simply cover the type with correction fluid or a small slip of paper before duplicating.

Making the Most of It!

BULLETIN BOARDS:

Creating clever bulletin boards for your classroom need not take fantastic amounts of time and money. With a little preparation and know-how you can have different boards each month with very little effort. Try some of these ideas:

1. Background paper should be put up only once a year. Choose colors that can go with many themes and holidays. A black butcher paper background will look terrific with springtime butterflies or a spooky Halloween display.

2. Butcher paper is not the only thing that can be used to cover the back of your board. You might like to try the classified ad section of the local newspaper for a current events board. Or how about colored burlap? Just fold it up at the end of the year to reuse again.

3. Wallpaper is another great background cover. Discontinued rolls can be purchased for next to nothing at discount hardware stores. Most can be wiped clean and will not fade like construction paper. (Do not glue wallpaper directly to the board, just staple or pin in place.)

ON-GOING
BULLETIN BOARDS:

Creating the on-going bulletin board can be easy. Give one of these ideas a try.

1. Choose one board to be a calendar display. Students can change this monthly. They can do the switching of dates, month titles and holiday symbols. Start the year with a great calendar board and with a few minor changes each month it will add a sparkle to the classroom.

2. A classroom tree bulletin board is another one that requires very little attention after September. Cut a large bare tree from brown butcher paper and display it in the center of the board. (Wood-grained adhesive paper makes a great tree, also.) Children can add fall leaves, flowers, apples, Christmas ornaments, birds, valentines, etc., to change the appearance each month.

ON-GOING
BULLETIN BOARDS:
(continued)

3. Birthday bulletin boards, classroom helpers, school announcement displays and reading group charts can all be created once before school starts and changed monthly with very little effort. With all these on-going ideas, you'll discover that all that bulletin board space seems smaller than you thought.

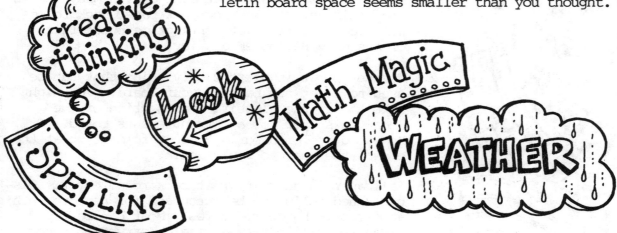

LETTERING AND
HEADINGS:

Not every school has a letter machine that produces perfect 2" or 4" letters from construction paper. (There is such a thing, you know.) The rest of us will just have to use the old stencil and scissor method. But wait, there is an easier way!

1. Don't cut individual letters. They are difficult to pin up straight, anyway. Instead, hand print bulletin board titles and headings onto strips of colored paper. When it is time for the board to come down, simply roll it up to use again next year.

   Use your imagination. Try cloud shapes and cartoon bubbles. They will all look great.

2. Hand lettering is not that difficult, even if your printing is not up to penmanship standards. Print block letters with a felt marker. Draw big dots at the ends of each letter. This will hide any mistakes and add a charming touch to the overall effect.

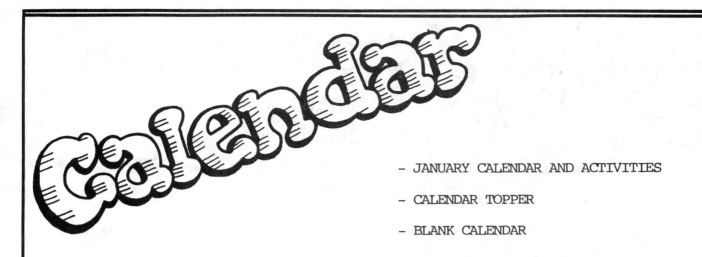

Calendar

- JANUARY CALENDAR AND ACTIVITIES

- CALENDAR TOPPER

- BLANK CALENDAR

January

I have a dream....

1   Today is NEW YEAR'S DAY! (Celebrate by asking your students to write New Year's resolutions!

2   BETSY ROSS, designer of the first American flag, was born on this day in 1752. (Ask students to find pictures of the various flags that have flown over our country.)

3   ALASKA became the United States 49th state in 1959. (Have your students find ten interesting facts about Alaska and then locate it on the classroom map.)

4   LOUIS BRAILLE, inventor of the blind alphabet, was born on this day in 1809. (Locate the Braille alphabet in the encyclopedia and have each child write his name in braille.)

5   Today is GEORGE WASHINGTON CARVER DAY! This multitalented man invented more than 300 different products. (Ask students to list some of his accomplishments.)

6   JOAN OF ARC was born on this day in 1412. She was burned at the stake for her religious beliefs. (Ask students to find out more about this courageous woman and report to the class.

7   Today marks the birthdate of MIGUEL HIDALGO, father of Mexican independence. (Ask students to find out how this man helped his countrymen defeat the Spaniards.)

8   ELVIS PRESLEY was born on this day in 1935. (Just for fun, play a couple of his songs during class exercise time.)

9   The first school of SEEING EYE DOGS was founded on this day in 1929. (Ask students to list the many reasons a blind person might appreciate having a Seeing Eye Dog.)

10   OIL was discovered in Texas on this day in 1901. (Ask students why this valuable resource is called "Black Gold.")

11   CIGARETTES were declared hazardous to our health on this day in 1964. (Have students list the various reasons people should not smoke.)

12   CHARLES PERRAULT, French writer and poet, was born on this day in 1628. Perrault wrote the famous tales of "Cinderella," "Puss and Boots" and "Little Red Riding Hood." (Read one of these stories to your class, in his honor.)

13   STEPHEN FOSTER, composer of more than 175 songs, was born on this day in 1826. (Join your class in a round of "Oh! Susanna" in celebration.)

14   Missionary and humanitarian, ALBERT SCHWEITZER, was born on this day in 1875. (Ask students to find out what great things this man did and what prize he was awarded.)

15   MARTIN LUTHER KING, American civil rights leader, was born on this day in 1929. (Read Dr. King's "I have a dream" speech to your class. Ask them to write about their "dream" for America.)

16   Today is NATIONAL NOTHING DAY! (Ask children to invent their own holiday for this day. Have them choose colors, symbols and reasons for their holiday and present their ideas to the class.)

17   BENJAMIN FRANKLIN, American statesman and inventor, was born on this day in 1706. (Fly a kite with your class in celebration of Franklin's discovery of electricity.)

18   American heavyweight boxing champion, MUHAMMAD ALI, was born on this day in 1942. (Ali often recited short rhymes about himself, such as; "I run like a butterfly and sting like a bee!" Ask students to make up their own rhymes about themselves.)

19   ROBERT E. LEE, American Civil War general, was born on this day in 1807. (Ask students to list the states that fought on the side of the South during the Civil War.)

20   Today is PRESIDENTIAL INAUGURATION DAY in the United States. This event happens every four years when the new President takes the oath of office. (Watch this historical event on television with your class.)

21   MARY BRENT, the first woman in America to ask for the right to vote, was born on this day in 1648. (Ask your students to find out how many years it took for her request to be granted.)

22   Today is "ELFSTEDENTOCHT" or the "Eleven Cities Race" in the Netherlands. Ice skaters race the 124 miles across the frozen canals of Holland. (Read Hans Brinker, by Mary Mapes Dodge, to your class in commemoration.)

23   JOHN HANCOCK, American patriot, was born on this day in 1737. (Ask students to locate a copy of the Declaration of Independence and then tell you why this man is so famous.)

January

24   GOLD was discovered in SUTTER'S MILL, California, in 1848. (Can your students find Sutter's Mill, (Sacramento) on the classroom map?)

25   The first WINTER OLYMPICS took place on this day in 1924 in Chamonix, France. (Ask students to list the various Winter Olympic events and write about which event they would like to compete in.)

26   DOUGLAS MACARTHUR, American WWII general, was born on this day in 1880. (Ask students to find out about his contribution and where he had promised to "return.")

27   WOLFGANG AMADEUS MOZART, Austrian composer, was born on this day in 1756. (Find a Mozart symphony and play it to your class during silent reading.)

28   The United States COAST GUARD was established on this day in 1915. (Ask students why we need this branch of the armed services to protect our coast.)

29   THOMAS PAINE, American political philosopher and writer, was born on this day in 1737. (Have students research the name of Paine's pamphlet that encouraged American independence.)

30   The LIBRARY OF CONGRESS began operating on this day in 1815. Today, it houses more than 80 million books! (Ask your students to find out which President's collection of 6,000 books began it all.)

31   HAM, a male chimpanzee, was rocketed into space during Project Mercury, in 1961. (Ask students how Ham helped the space program of the United States.)

CHINESE NEW YEAR – Between the middle of January and early
                 March. (The first day of the new moon
                 using the Chinese calendar.)

JANUARY

January

sun	mon	tue	wed	thu	fri	sat

Winter Activities

- BOOKMARKS
- AWARDS AND CERTIFICATES
- PENCIL TOPPERS
- MY WINTER BOOK
- SNOWMAN WHEEL
- SNOWFLAKES
- MATCHING MITTENS
- PENGUIN POEM PAGE

JANUARY

Bookmarks

warm up with a good book this winter!

from the Library

Happy New Year!

Discover the wonder of winter at the Library!

JANUARY

January Awards

Happy New Year!

_____
Name

IS HAVING A
GREAT YEAR!

_____
Date

_____
Teacher

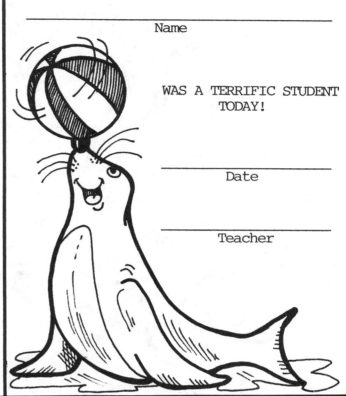

_____
Name

WAS A TERRIFIC STUDENT
TODAY!

_____
Date

_____
Teacher

_____
Name

WAS A REAL JOY
IN CLASS TODAY!

_____
Date

_____
Teacher

_____
Name

WAS A BIG HELP TODAY!

_____
Date

_____
Teacher

Pencil Toppers

Reproduce these "Pencil Toppers" onto construction or index paper. Color and cut out. Use an art knife to cut through the Xs.

Slide a pencil through both Xs, as shown.

Give them as classroom awards or birthday treats.

JANUARY

My
Winter
Book

_____
Name

Snowman Wheel

CUT
OUT

CUT
OUT

JANUARY

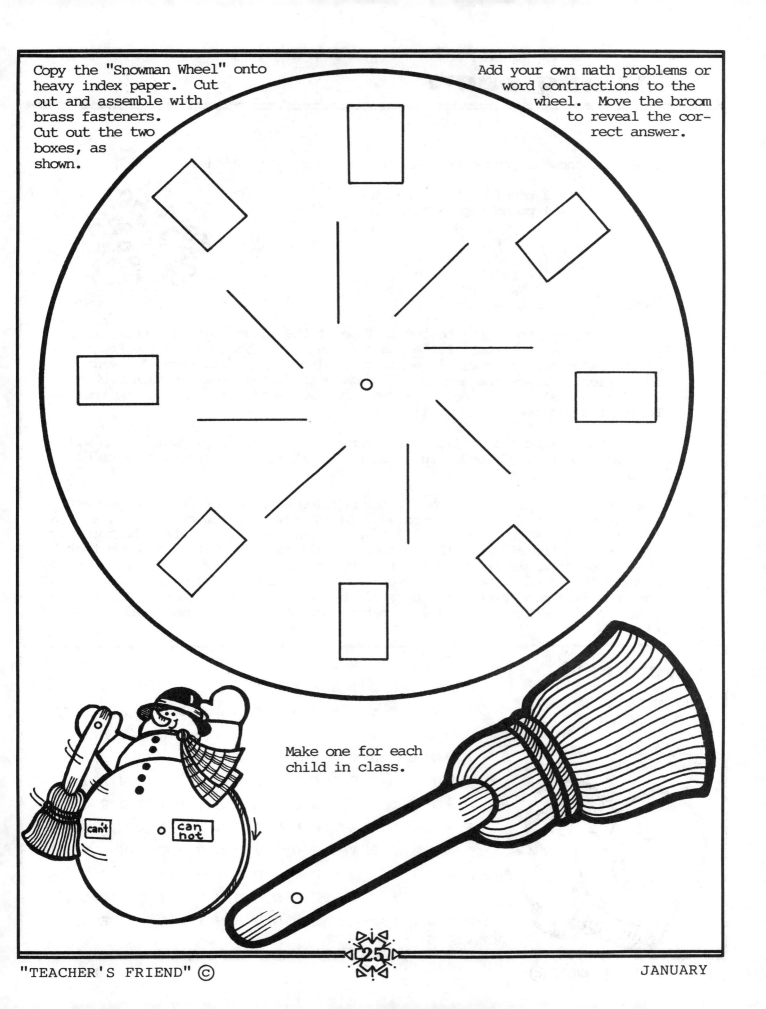

Copy the "Snowman Wheel" onto heavy index paper. Cut out and assemble with brass fasteners. Cut out the two boxes, as shown.

Add your own math problems or word contractions to the wheel. Move the broom to reveal the correct answer.

Make one for each child in class.

can't   can not

Making Snow

Make real snow in your classroom with these simple materials.

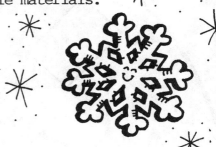

    1 - 3 pound empty coffee can
    1 - 1 pound empty coffee can
    1 - bag of crushed ice
    1 - small terrycloth towel
        rock salt
        1/2 pound dry ice
        sharp knife
        masking tape

Wrap the towel around the bottom portion of the larger can and secure in place with masking tape. Put a small amount of crushed ice in the bottom of the large can and sprinkle generously with salt. (Use about 1/3 salt to 2/3 ice.) Place the smaller can inside the larger and continue packing the ice and salt in the space between the two cans. Fill the ice to the top of the outside of the small can.

By breathing into the small can you can now illustrate how your breath will condense and form a cloud. This cloud is just like the clouds on a cold winter day.

Next, comes the dry ice. The dry ice must be handled carefully to prevent burns. Pick the dry ice up with a cloth and scrape a few grains of ice into the cloud with a sharp knife. Ice crystals will soon start to form. Point out to the students that these crystals are just like the seeds that start snowstorms in the winter. Breathe again into the small can continuing to make the cloud. The new moisture you are adding with your breath will continue to freeze around the crystals making them larger each time. Before long, your students will realize that the crystals have become real snow-flakes!

Word Find

FIND THESE WINTER WORDS
IN THE PUZZLE: SNOW, ICE,
MITTENS, WINTER, FROST,
COLD, JACKET, SLED, ICICLE,
SNOWFLAKE, SKI, SNOWMAN.

```
C M D F G S N O W M A N D R T F G T Y H J U
M D E F R G T S K I B H Y N F D R V B N M F
I G H J D F G H J G T H Y J R D T G H J K L
T D C V W I N T E R D C X Z O F T H J K L O
T D F G H J T H Y G H J K U S L E D D S A E
E M N B V C F T F C D R F C T S D A W E I K
N S D D F G V B H O J M K H V F T R D R C V
S N O W F L A K E L V C S W E S A X C Z E V
A X C V B Y T G H D S V B N H Y U J K L T S
A S X C J A C K E T S D F V B H Y T G F E S
A S D F F G T R E C N K L M N S I C I C L E
A X D R T A C V S N O W B H Y T G F D E W S
```

Snowflakes

They say no two snowflakes are alike. See how many different snowflakes your class can make using this simple pattern.

Cut the circle from white typing paper and fold in half. Fold again in thirds, as shown. Cut designs on both sides of the pie shaped piece. Unfold the paper to see your beautiful new snowflake.

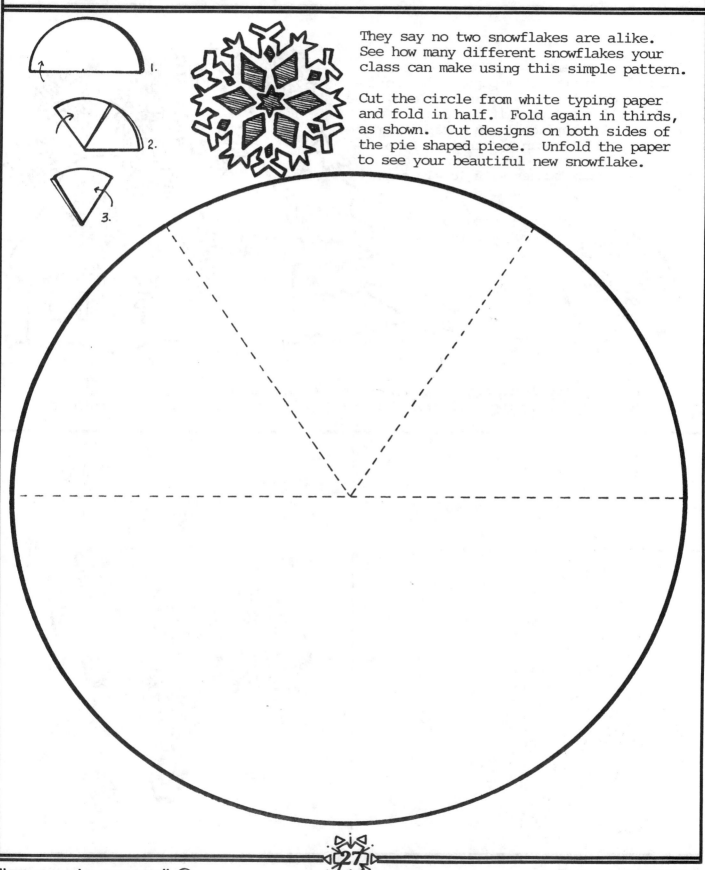

SNOW SCENES

Have each student draw a snow scene on
dark blue construction paper using colored
chalk. When the drawing is complete, give
each child a potato half and ask him to
cut the flat surface in the shape of a snowflake. Children can dip their potato designs into white poster paint and decorate their snow scenes with lovely snow-
flakes.

Cut the potato so that
the snowflake is raised.

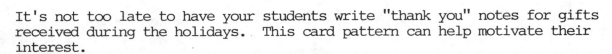

It's not too late to have your students write "thank you" notes for gifts
received during the holidays. This card pattern can help motivate their
interest.

Matching Mittens

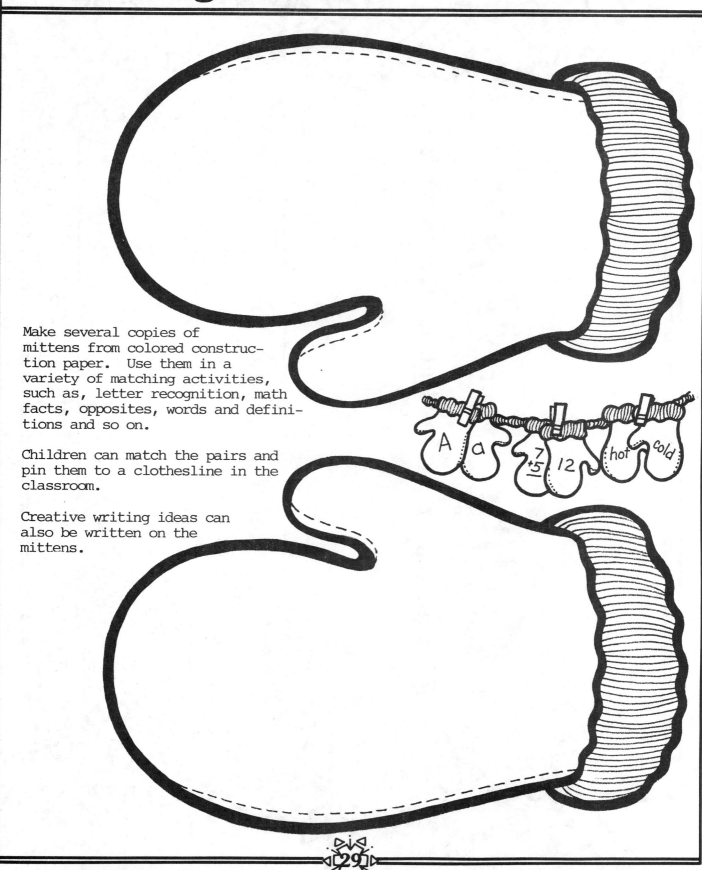

Make several copies of mittens from colored construction paper. Use them in a variety of matching activities, such as, letter recognition, math facts, opposites, words and definitions and so on.

Children can match the pairs and pin them to a clothesline in the classroom.

Creative writing ideas can also be written on the mittens.

Certificate of Award

This award of distinction is presented to

_____

in recognition of

_____

_____

Date _____

CONGRATULATIONS !

This is to certify that

_____

has accomplished

_____

_____

Date _____ Teacher _____

NEAT   PRINTING   AWARD

_____

has demonstrated
neat printing!

_____

_____

Teacher _____
Date _____

Penguin Poem

NAME

JANUARY

- CALENDAR WHEELS

- MY BOOK OF MONTHS

- MONTHS OF THE YEAR WORD FIND

- SEASON SYMBOLS

Calendar Wheels

These clever "Calendar Wheels" are easy to make and especially fun for the students to change each day of the year.

Cut four 8 inch circles from colored posterboard. Cut out each calendar wheel and glue to the posterboard circles. Laminate if you wish. Attach the wheels to a full sheet of posterboard with brass fasteners. Glue the appropriate arrows to the board, as shown.

Display the "Calendar Wheels" on the class bulletin board or make copies for each child in class and let them make their own "Calendar Wheels" to take home. This is a wonderful way to reinforce the concepts of seasons, months, dates, days of the week and weather changes.

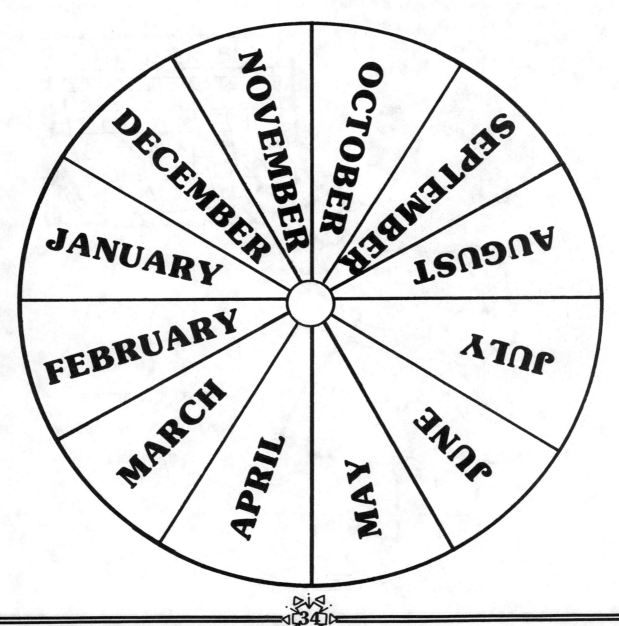

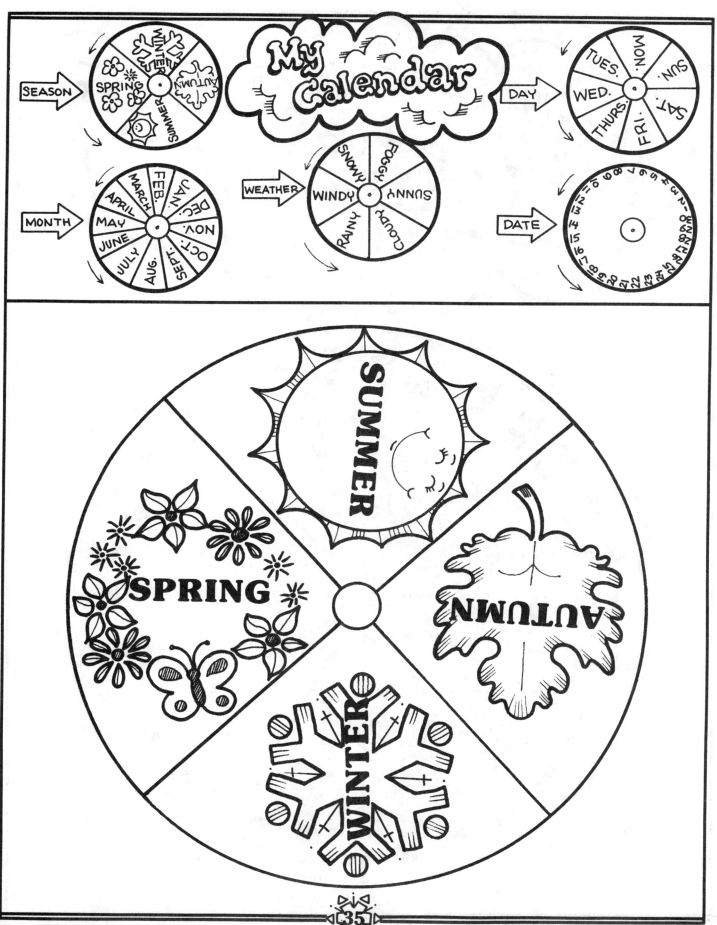

JANUARY

"TEACHER'S FRIEND" ©

JANUARY

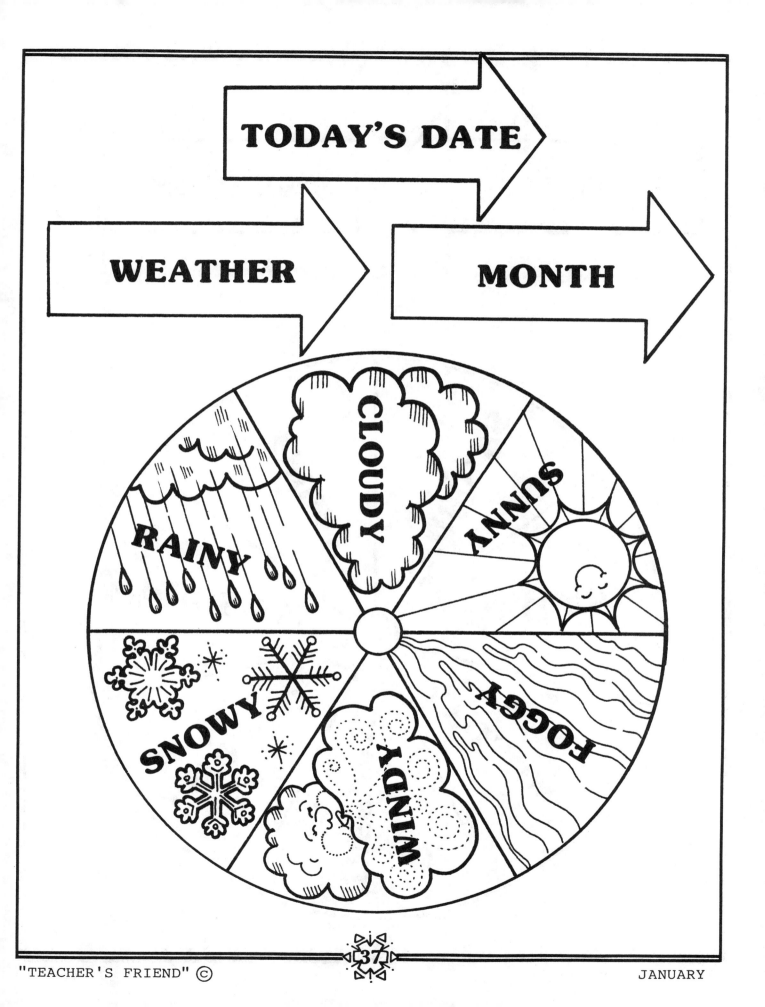

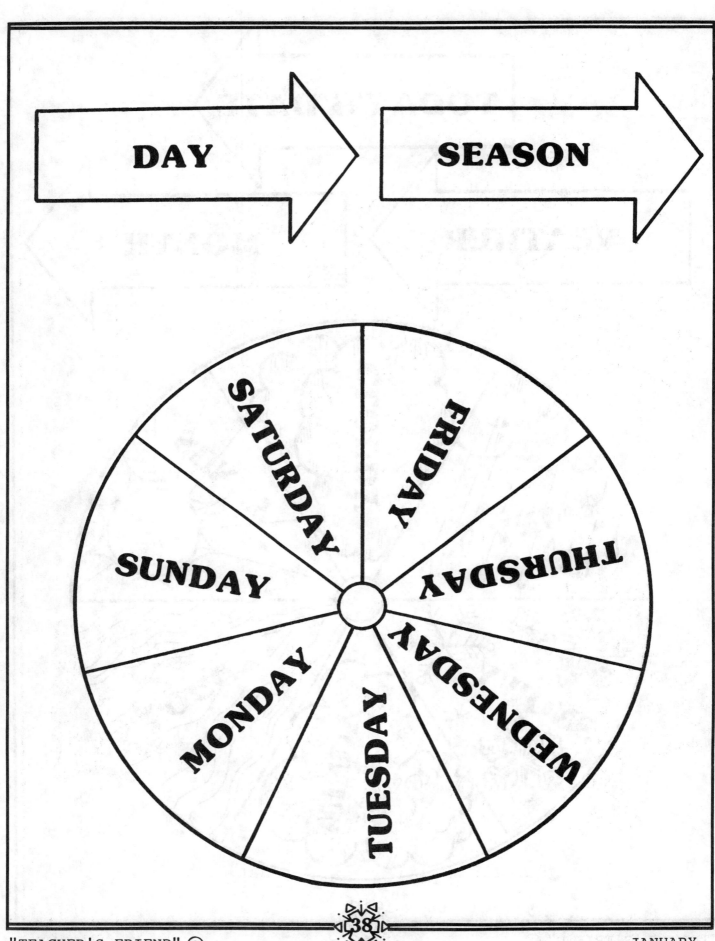

JANUARY

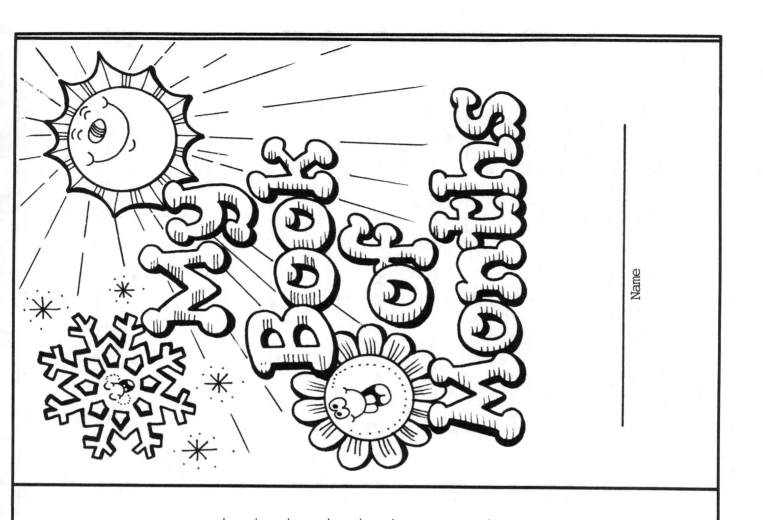

My Book of Months

Name _____

My favorite

My favorite month is: _____

Because _____
_____

My favorite season is: _____

Because _____
_____

I completed my Book of Months on this date: _____
_____

The End

February

February is the _____ month.

February has _____ days.

I like February because: _____
_____

These people have birthdays in February.
_____
_____

Here are three words that describe February.

1. _____

2. _____

3. _____

My favorite holiday in February is: _____
_____

January

January is the _____ month.

January has _____ days.

I like January because: _____
_____

These people have birthdays in January.
_____
_____

Here are three words that describe January.

1. _____

2. _____

3. _____

My favorite holiday in January is: _____
_____

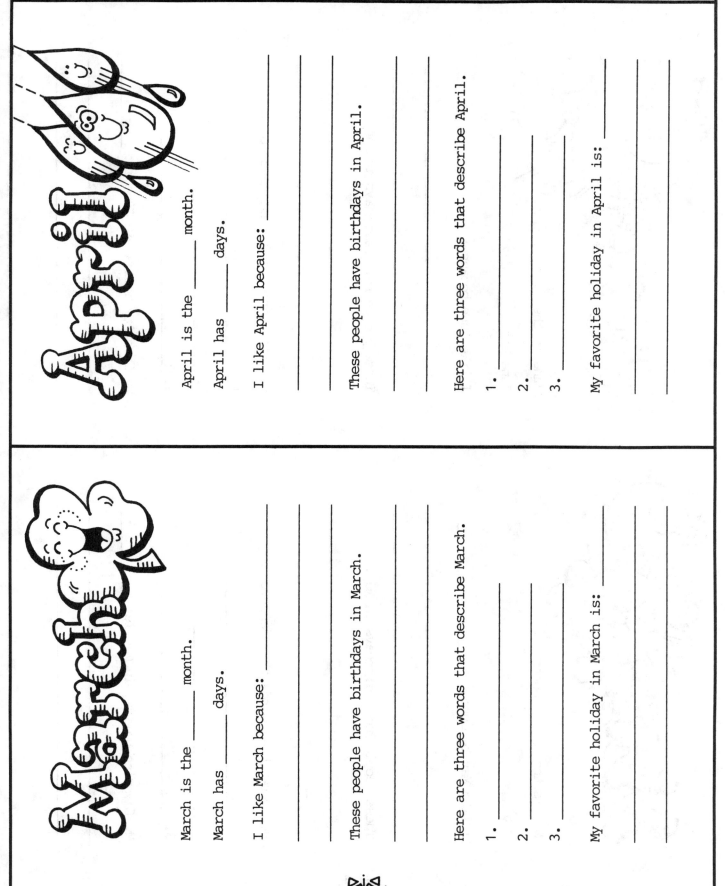

March

March is the _____ month.

March has _____ days.

I like March because: _____

These people have birthdays in March. _____

Here are three words that describe March.

1. _____

2. _____

3. _____

My favorite holiday in March is: _____

April

April is the _____ month.

April has _____ days.

I like April because: _____

These people have birthdays in April. _____

Here are three words that describe April.

1. _____

2. _____

3. _____

My favorite holiday in April is: _____

June

June is the _____ month.

June has _____ days.

I like June because: _____

_____

These people have birthdays in June.

_____

Here are three words that describe June.

1. _____

2. _____

3. _____

My favorite holiday in June is: _____

May

May is the _____ month.

May has _____ days.

I like May because: _____

_____

These people have birthdays in May.

_____

Here are three words that describe May.

1. _____

2. _____

3. _____

My favorite holiday in May is: _____

August

August is the _____ month.

August has _____ days.

I like August because: _____
_____
_____

These people have birthdays in August. _____
_____

Here are three words that describe August.

1. _____

2. _____

3. _____

My favorite holiday in August is: _____
_____

July

July is the _____ month.

July has _____ days.

I like July because: _____
_____
_____

These people have birthdays in July. _____
_____

Here are three words that describe July.

1. _____

2. _____

3. _____

My favorite holiday in July is: _____
_____

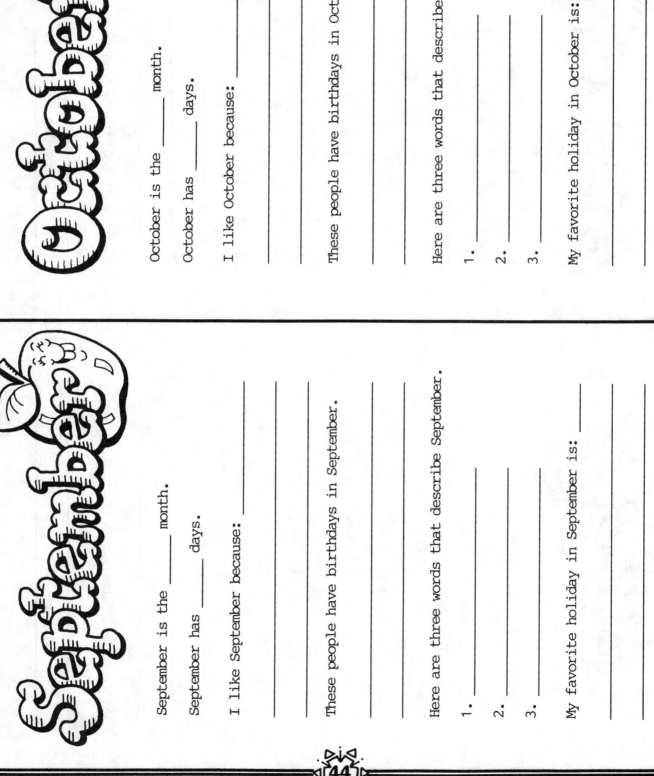

October

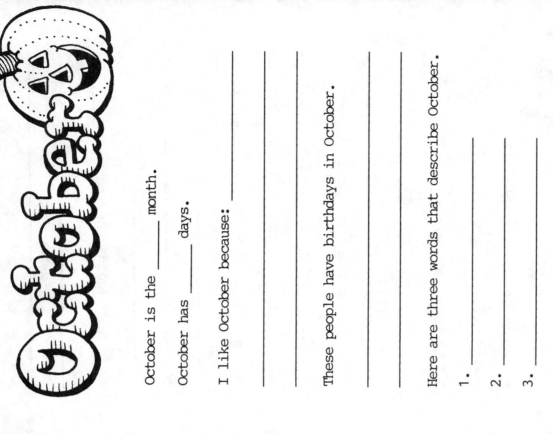

October is the _____ month.

October has _____ days.

I like October because: _____

_____

_____

These people have birthdays in October.

_____

_____

Here are three words that describe October.

1. _____

2. _____

3. _____

My favorite holiday in October is: _____

_____

September

September is the _____ month.

September has _____ days.

I like September because: _____

_____

_____

These people have birthdays in September.

_____

_____

Here are three words that describe September.

1. _____

2. _____

3. _____

My favorite holiday in September is: _____

_____

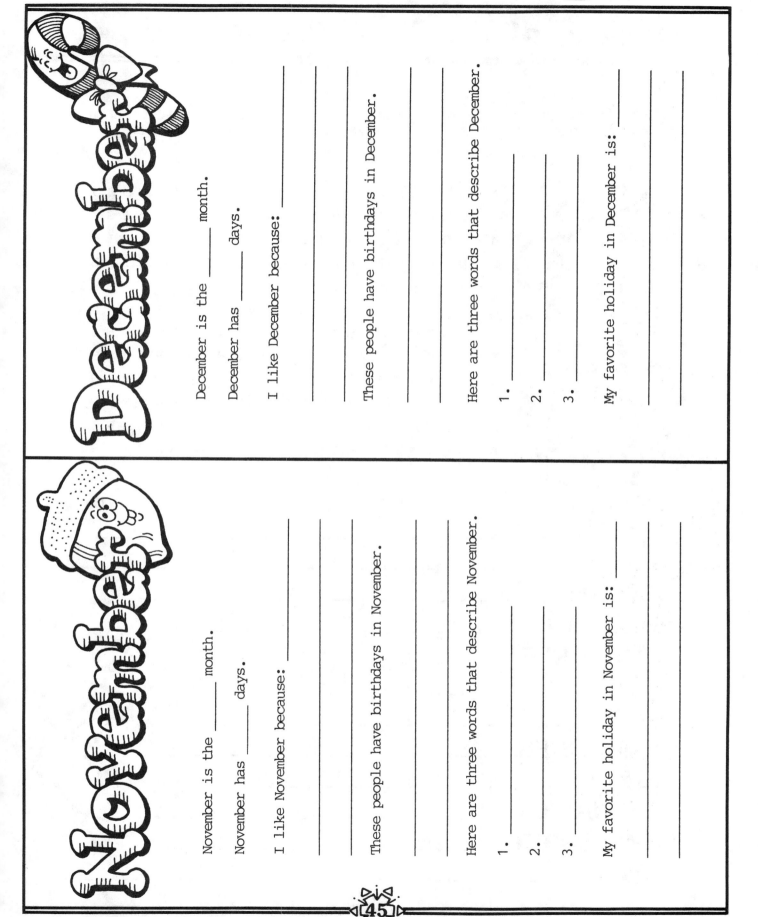

December

December is the _____ month.

December has _____ days.

I like December because: _____

_____

_____

These people have birthdays in December.

_____

_____

Here are three words that describe December.

1. _____

2. _____

3. _____

My favorite holiday in December is: _____

_____

November

November is the _____ month.

November has _____ days.

I like November because: _____

_____

_____

These people have birthdays in November.

_____

_____

Here are three words that describe November.

1. _____

2. _____

3. _____

My favorite holiday in November is: _____

_____

Months of the Year Word Find

ACTIVITY 3

FIND THE MONTHS OF THE YEAR IN THE PUZZLE BELOW: JANUARY, FEBRUARY, MARCH, APRIL, MAY, JUNE, JULY, AUGUST, SEPTEMBER, OCTOBER, NOVEMBER, DECEMBER.

```
A M S D F R E T G D C Q A S E D F R G B N M C D S J
A X C M A R C H A C F V B G H N J U N E O U K I G A
A S S D E F R T G J S D E R T G B N H J U K I L I N
P S D S E P T E M B E R F G H Y J U K I O L G T D U
R D F G T H Y J U D F R T G H Y N J U G C H Y U G A
I S W E D C V G T D E C E M B E R D R F T S W A W R
L S X C V B G F D S A W E R T G Y A D E O F R S E Y
X S A F R E T Y H G T R E D C F G T R A B R G H J S
G J U L Y A X M Z S E R C V G T H Y A R E F G V B N
X Z C V B G T A A N O V E M B E R K L E R A S E D F
A W S D F R C Y A S D C V F G D C V F G A U G U S T
A S X F E B R U A R Y C V B H J K L O P M N G F D S
```

ACTIVITY 4

BDREECEM _____

TUUSGA _____

CMRAH _____

TEROOCB _____

RYUABRFE _____

NEUJ _____

RLPAI _____

VMEONREB _____

AMY _____

UYNJAAR _____

PMEESRBET _____

LJYU _____

Now, unsramble the months.

JANUARY

Months of the Year

January is... _____

_____

February is... _____

_____

March is... _____

_____

April is... _____

_____

May is... _____

_____

June is... _____

_____

July is... _____

_____

August is... _____

_____

September is... _____

_____

October is... _____

_____

November is... _____

_____

December is... _____

_____

Write a sentence or a simile describing each month.

Season Symbols

JANUARY

New Year's Day

January 1st

- NEW YEAR'S DAY CUSTOMS
- NEW YEAR'S DAY WORD FIND
- NEW YEAR'S RESOLUTIONS
- HAPPY NEW YEAR BOOK
- CREATIVE WRITING BELL
- HAPPY NEW YEAR VISOR

New Year's Day Customs

The custom of celebrating the New Year on January 1st began over 2,000 years ago in Rome, Italy. The Romans had previously celebrated March 25th, the vernal equinox, as the beginning of the New Year. Government officials were elected in December and assumed their new positions on the day before January 1st. Gradually, citizens began celebrating this first day as the beginning of the New Year. However, this change created confusion in the Roman calendar. The months of September, October, November and December, which refer to the seventh, eighth, ninth and tenth months of the year were now the ninth, tenth, eleventh and twelfth months. By changing the New Year to January, these month's names had little meaning.

In 45 B.C., Julius Caesar, the Roman emperor, selected the name "January" for the first month of the year. This name was chosen to honor the Roman god, Janus. It was believed that this god had two faces looking in opposite directions. In his right hand he held a key to unlock the door to the future and keep locked the door to the past. In his left hand he held a scepter, as a symbol of power and authority.

The Senate of Rome awarded Julius Caesar a month of his own for his successful transfer of the New Year and his improvement of the Roman calendar. We call this month "July."

New Year's Day, today, is celebrated many different ways in many different countries. Here are a few examples of celebrations in other lands:

GERMANY - The people of Germany enjoy a custom called "lead pouring." On New Year's Day, youngsters drop hot drops of melted lead into containers of cold water. As the lead cools and hardens, unusual shapes appear. The children have fun telling their fortunes by the shapes of the lead. If the lead shape resembles a coin, they might look forward to obtaining money.

ROSH HASHANA - The Jewish New Year is a quiet time for meditation and prayer. This is a holy date to the Jewish people, considered the birthday of the world. Each person asks forgiveness from God and vows to live a better life. Rosh Hashana is celebrated on the first day of the Jewish calendar, in September or October.

SWEDEN - The Swedish people celebrate the New Year with parties and family gatherings on the last night of the year. There is much food and merrymaking. Friendship and good wishes are expressed to one and all.

AUSTRIA - Ever since 1936, the Austrian government has commemorated the New Year with the minting of good luck tokens called "Gluecksmenze." New Year wishes are engraved on one side of the coin and good luck symbols on the other. Austrians also enjoy eating New Year's candies in the shape of good luck pigs.

New Year's Day Word Find

NIGERIA - The people of northern Nigeria celebrate the New Year at the beginning of fishing season, usually the first part of February. Thousands of people gather along the banks of the Sokoto River with fish nets in hand. At a given signal, everyone jumps in the water, startling the fish into the nets. The fisherman with the largest fish, wins a prize.

SEMINOLE NEW YEAR - For four days, during the month of July, the Seminole Indians of Florida celebrate the harvest of new corn as the beginning of the New Year. The first day, they play games, feast and dance. On the second day, the men of the tribe begin a fast. Everyone dances the Green Corn Dance on the third evening and gives prayers of thanks for the good harvest. The fourth day, the men break their fast and eat the new corn of the New Year.

UNITED STATES - In our own country, the old year is symbolized by an old man, Father Time, and the New Year is represented by a baby in diapers. In the southern states, it is customary to eat certain foods on New Year's Day in hopes of prosperity through the coming year. Black-eyed peas symbolize pennies and greens represent dollar bills. Making New Year's resolutions is a relatively new custom based on the idea of improving the New Year in hopes it will be better than the last.

ACTIVITY 2

FIND THESE NEW YEAR WORDS IN THE PUZZLE BELOW: JANUARY, NEW YEAR, BELLS, CELEBRATE, MIDNIGHT, FATHER TIME, RESOLUTION, CONFETTI, BALLOONS, CUSTOM, FRIENDS.

```
G N M K L O P L K M J N H G A S W E R T X
A S W D V F R T F V G E S E D F T G H Y U
F R I E N D S X D R T W U I C F T G B N B
Q E S D F R G T G H N Y F R C U S T O M N
A S E R C V B N H Y T E W S C V F R G D J
A O C V B C O N D V F A F R B D E R T Y Y
X L C O N F E T T I D R S E E C V B N M I
Q U X C V B G F D E B A E F L A S D E R U
A T D F G H X E R T Y H C E L E B R A T E
Z I X C V G T F R E D F G T S D V B N M U
A O F B N M J K F A T H E R T I M E X C T
W N S D B A L L O O N S C D R E T G H Y N
M I D N I G H T V D E R T F G R D S W E R
A S D E W Q X C V J A N U A R Y N H J K L
```

New Year's Resolutions

During the New Year's celebrations, we often pledge to make the coming year better than the last. Many people make New Year's resolutions. Think of some resolutions you might make and write them in the spaces below.

List your resolutions for becoming a better.....

STUDENT _____

_____

_____

BROTHER OR SISTER _____

_____

_____

SON OR DAUGHTER _____

_____

_____

FRIEND _____

_____

_____

If you could make a New Year's resolution for our country or the world, what would it be?

_____

_____

_____

JANUARY

Have each child
make a Happy New
Year Book using this
pattern. Ask them to report
on New Year's Day customs or
write their own resolutions.

Creative Writing

Give each student a bell and bell handle cut from construction paper.

Ask them to read the story starter on the handle and write a creative story on the bell. The handle can be glued to the bell when finished and displayed on the board.

_____
Name

AS THE CLOCK STRUCK 12 O'CLOCK MIDNIGHT ON NEW YEAR'S EVE, THE LIGHTS SUDDENLY WENT OFF!

_____
Name

DURING THE NEW YEAR'S PARTY, I THREW CONFETTI HIGH INTO THE AIR! GUESS WHERE IT LANDED?

_____
Name

THE CAR HORN STUCK AT MIDNIGHT ON NEW YEAR'S EVE, WAKING EVERY DOG IN THE NEIGHBORHOOD!

_____
Name

I FELL ASLEEP FIVE MINUTES BEFORE MIDNIGHT ON NEW YEAR'S EVE, MISSING THE MOST EXCITING NIGHT OF MY LIFE!

Visor

Copy this "Happy New Year" visor onto sturdy index or construction paper. Children can do the coloring.

Punch holes at both ends and attach string elastic or mailing string. (With elastic, the students can easily remove the visors without retyping.)

Chinese New Year

- LANTERN AND FISH KITE
- NEW YEAR'S DRAGON
- FORTUNE COOKIES
- CHINESE ZODIAC

- DRAGON GAMEBOARD
- INTERNATIONAL CHILDREN
- TANGRAM
- CREATIVE WRITING

Chinese New Year

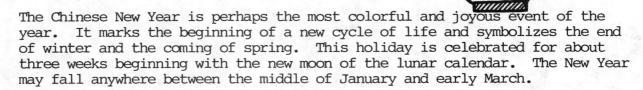 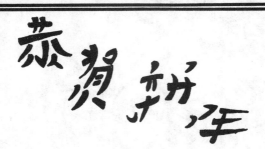

The Chinese New Year is perhaps the most colorful and joyous event of the year. It marks the beginning of a new cycle of life and symbolizes the end of winter and the coming of spring. This holiday is celebrated for about three weeks beginning with the new moon of the lunar calendar. The New Year may fall anywhere between the middle of January and early March.

The last days of the old year are very busy for Chinese families. All the food for the festive celebrations must be prepared in advance. It is considered bad luck to use a knife or sharp tool during the first few days of the New Year, for fear of "cutting" the New Year's luck. All debts must be paid and accounting books brought up-to-date before the end of the year.

Cleaning the house is especially important during this time. Evil spirits must be dusted and swept out of the house. After all the evil spirits are chased away, it is time to say good-bye to the Kitchen God, Tsao Chuen. His spirit has been residing in the home during the past year. He takes notes about the family and reports his finding to the Jade Emperor. On the twenty-third day of the twelfth month, the family honors the Kitchen God with a farewell dinner. The meal usually consists of sweet foods in hopes of encouraging him to report only kind things to the Emperor. After the ceremonial feast, children light firecrackers to keep evil spirits away until Tsao Chuen's return on New Year's Eve.

On the eve of the New Year, after all preparations are ready, the outer door to the house is sealed with red paper to prevent good luck from leaving the house.

New Year's Day is a time for the entire family to gather for a feast of rice pudding, vegetarian dishes and pastries. The New Year marks the birthday of every family member. Before midnight, children receive good luck money in even numbered amounts, wrapped in small red envelopes. Everyone wears their newest clothes. Only kind words must be thought or spoken.

The Feast of the Lanterns is celebrated on the third day of the New Year. Lanterns of all shapes, sizes and colors decorate the streets and homes. Many cities hold fantastic parades, led by a huge dragon, the symbol of good luck. The dragon is made of bamboo and covered with silk and paper. More than fifty people have been known to support him as he weaves up and down the streets. Musicians, dancers and acrobats accompany the dragon in the parade. The festive celebration ends with a great fireworks display.

Lantern and Fish Kite

Make dozens of Chinese Lanterns by simply having each student fold a 12" X 18" sheet of colored construction paper in half and cut as shown. Ask them to unfold the paper and staple the outside edges to form a cylinder. Students can add paper handles and cut-paper decorations if they wish. Hang them throughout your classroom for a truly festive atmosphere.

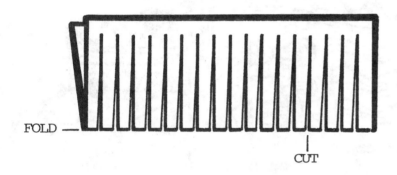

FOLD —

CUT

These gorgeous Fish Kites are fun to run with in the wind and make a beautiful bulletin board display.

Give each child a piece of butcher paper measuring about 36 inches long. Ask them to fold the paper in half, trace their fish pattern and cut it out.

Students can staple or glue the edges of their two fish shapes together, leaving the tail and mouth open. Children will love decorating their kites with crayons, paints, glitter and markers. Crepe paper streamers can also be added.

Fold the mouth of the kite inward a couple of times and shape it into a round opening. Attach kite string or yarn to the opening, as shown.

New Year's Dragon

On the third day of the New Year, a Feast of Lanterns is held throughout China. Lanterns of all shapes, colors and sizes are hung along the streets and in the family homes. That evening, a wonderful parade, led by the New Year's Dragon, takes place down the city's busiest street.

According to Chinese legend, the Dragon is not a horrible monster but rather a defender against evil spirits. He is the symbol of goodness and strength. This great New Year's Dragon is made of silk and paper and brightly painted. The head is a large mask, made of papier-mache and bamboo. The men of the town put on the Dragon costume and weave up and down the street, puffing smoke as spectators light firecrackers.

Your students can make their own New Year's Dragon with a few simple materials and imagination.

Cover a large cardboard box with bright colored paper. Cut another box in half, or use two box lids, and cover them with paper, also. Insert the two halves into an open end of the first box and glue in place, as shown in the illustration. Decorate with colored paper, glitter, tempera paint, etc.

Long sections of colored butcher paper can be used for the Dragon's tail. Staple the top edge of two sections of butcher paper and add a spiney paper ridge or fringe. Glue the tail to the back of the Dragon's head. (The Dragon's tail can be made as long as you like, depending on how many children will be inside the costume.) Decorate the tail in the same way as the head.

Children ringing bells and tapping tambourines can provide the music for your parade. Other children can hold class-made paper lanterns during the procession. No doubt about it, your Chinese New Year parade will be the hit of the school!

Fortune Cookies

Chinese Fortune Cookies are easy to make and especially fun during Chinese New Year celebrations.

Begin, by asking each student to write a fortune or saying on a small strip of typing paper and fold it in half.

Assign two or three students to measure the following ingredients:

8 egg whites
2 cups of sugar
1 cup melted butter
1 cup flour
1 teaspoon vanilla
1/2 teaspoon salt
4 tablespoons water

Separate the egg whites and beat them until they form stiff peaks. Blend in the sugar and butter. Discard the yolks. Add the flour, vanilla, salt and water to the mixture until it is smooth. Grease a cookie sheet and spoon the batter into 3 inch circles. Bake at 375° for about 8 minutes.

When the cookies are done, remove them with a pancake turner onto waxed paper. Place a fortune in the center of each circle and fold the cookie in half. Bend the cookies gently in the center, as shown. (If the cookies become to difficult to bend, put them back in the oven for a minute.)

Children will be delighted to select a cookie and read their special fortune written by a fellow classmate.

Note: The recipe does not work well with microwave ovens.

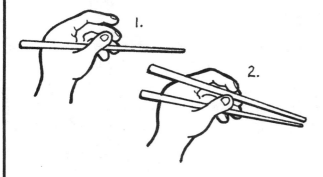

Place one chopstick firmly between the forefinger and thumb. Move the top stick up and down against the lower stick to grasp food.

SCRAMBLED CHINESE EGGS

Heat 2 tablespoons of oil and saute 1/2 minced onion in a frying pan or wok. Beat six or eight eggs with 2 teaspoons of soy sauce and add to the onions. Stir over medium heat until the eggs are cooked. Serve with stir-fried snowpeas, bean sprouts and bamboo shoots.

The main food in the Chinese diet is rice. Prepare enough rice for everyone in class and serve it in paper cups with chopsticks. (Many grocery stores carry disposable chopsticks in economical packages.)

Chinese Zodiac

YEAR OF THE DRAGON   (1952, 1964, 1976, 1988)

People born under the sign of the Dragon have been given the gifts of courage, health and gentleness. They are good rulers and sensitive to others.

YEAR OF THE SNAKE   (1953, 1965, 1977, 1989)

People born under this sign possess great wisdom. They are fortunate in money matters and are very handsome or beautiful.

YEAR OF THE HORSE   (1954, 1966, 1978, 1990)

Those born under the sign of the Horse are very cheerful and popular with others. They are good with their hands and quite talented.

YEAR OF THE RAM   (1955, 1967, 1979, 1991)

People born under this sign are very artistic and enjoy beautiful things. They are most happy when doing creative tasks.

YEAR OF THE MONKEY   (1956, 1968, 1980, 1992)

Monkey people are good decision makers and have great common sense. They are quite successful and keep themselves well-informed.

YEAR OF THE ROOSTER   (1957, 1969, 1981, 1993)

People born under this sign are outspoken and deep thinkers. They are devoted to their work and attract loyal friends.

JANUARY

Chinese Zodiac

YEAR OF THE DOG   (1958, 1970, 1982, 1994)

Those born under the Dog sign are extremely
loyal and honest. They have a deep sense of
justice and duty and can always keep a secret.

YEAR OF THE BOAR   (1959, 1971, 1983, 1995)

People born under this sign have a strong
inner strength and are very brave. They are
shy, courteous and make friends for life.

YEAR OF THE RAT   (1960, 1972, 1984, 1996)

People born under the sign of the Rat have
great charm. They are known for their ambi-
tion, integrity and drive.

YEAR OF THE OX   (1961, 1973, 1985, 1997)

Ox people are very patient and are good
listeners. They inspire others with their
calm assuredness.

YEAR OF THE TIGER   (1962, 1974, 1986, 1998)

Tiger people are considered very good friends.
They are careful planners and are respected
by others.

YEAR OF THE HARE   (1963, 1975, 1987, 1999)

Persons born under the sign of the Hare are
blessed with good fortune and seldom lose their
tempers. They always keep their promises.

JANUARY

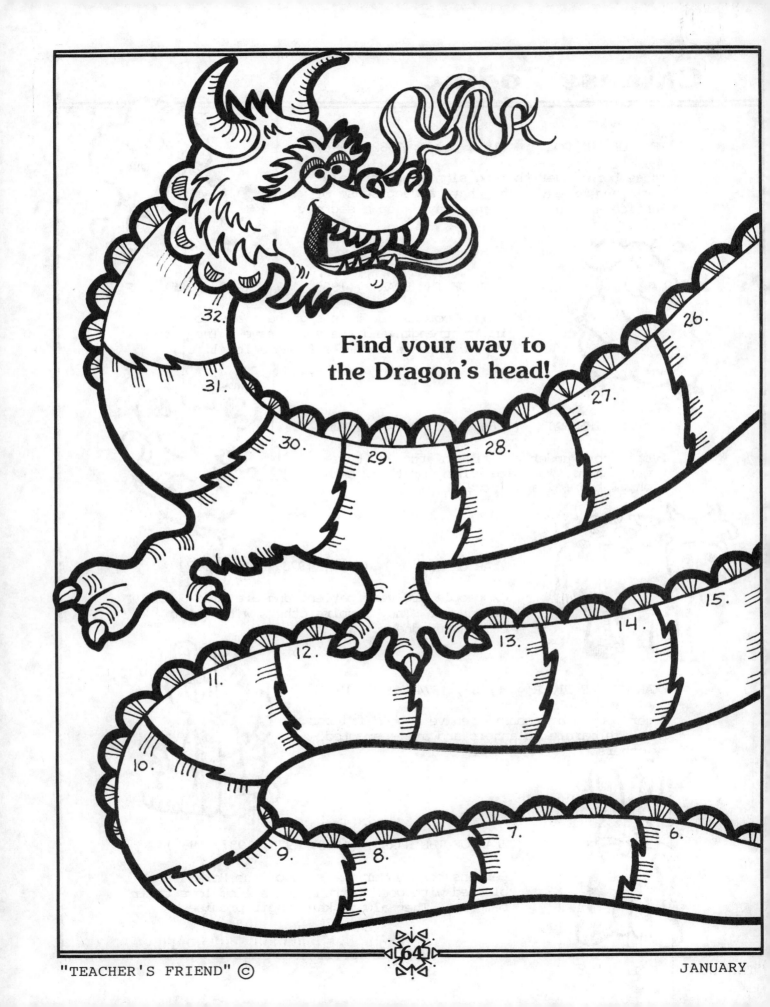

Find your way to
the Dragon's head!

Assemble both pages on poster board to make a fun Chinese New Year gameboard.

TEACHERS: Two, three or four children can play this game. Make your own task cards or write math problems, that must be solved, on each dragon section.

     JANUARY

JANUARY

Tangram

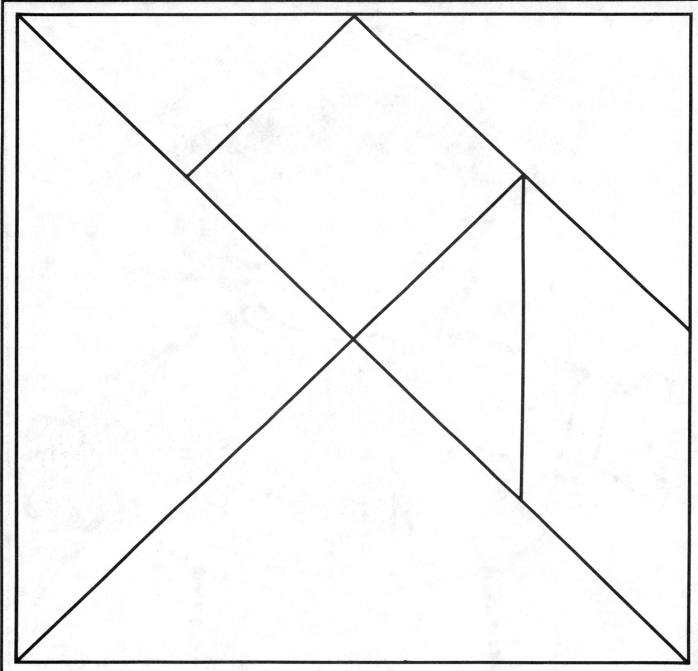

A Tangram is an ancient Chinese puzzle cut from a square piece of paper. It consists of five triangles, a parallelogram and a small square. These seven shapes can be combined to form many different shapes and designs.

Give each of your students a copy of the Tangram. Have them cut out the pieces and arrange them on a contrasting colored sheet of paper. Glue the shapes in place and display the best Tangrams on the class board.

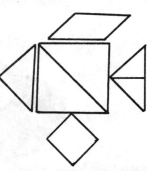

JANUARY

Happy "Chinese" New Year

GUNG

"HAPPY"

HAY

FAT

"NEW"

CHOY

"YEAR"

Children will love speaking and writing Chinese during Chinese New Year celebrations. Ask students to pronounce the words "Kung Shi" (Gung She) which means "Happy New Year." Traditionally, this greeting is said to friends with hands folded and bowing at the waist. After the children have perfected their greeting, have them try their hand at writing the characters "Gung Hay Fat Choy" on New Year banners.

Cut long rectangles, about 12" X 30", of red butcher paper and ask students to write the characters "Gung Hay Fat Choy" down the center of the banners with black tempera paint.

After the banners have dried, cut 12" strips of black construction paper. Fold the strips over long pieces of yarn and staple to the top of the banners.

Hang these lovely Chinese greetings in your classroom throughout your New Year celebrations.

JANUARY

Creative Writing

Dr. Martin Luther King

Martin Luther King Day

January 15th

- I HAVE A DREAM....

- DR. MARTIN LUTHER KING PORTRAIT

- I HAVE A DREAM PLEDGE

- DREAM MOBILE

- BROTHERHOOD

Dr. Martin Luther King

No one person in the history of Black America has inspired a nation as did Dr. Martin Luther King, Jr. He has been one of the country's most dynamic leaders in the fight for peaceful equality of all men.

Martin Luther King was born on January 15, 1929, in Atlanta, Georgia. His father was a well known minister of one of Atlanta's leading black churches. In 1947, he was ordained a Baptist minister and later accepted the pastor-ship of Dexter Avenue Baptist Church in Montgomery, Alabama. In 1953, he married Coretta Scott and together they raised four children.

During the 1950's, Martin Luther King became a leader in the Civil Rights Movement overtaking the South. His first challenge was the boycotting of buses in Montgomery, Alabama. Mrs. Rosa Parks, a black seamstress, re-fused to give up her bus seat to a white passenger. The arrest of Mrs. Parks triggered the 382 day boycott by black passengers. Many of the whites blamed Dr. King for the success of the boycott and threats on his life be-came very real when a bomb exploded on his family's front porch. However, Dr. King stood fast in his conviction of non-violence and urged his people to forgive their enemies and achieve a peaceful solution to their problems. The bus boycott was recognized as a clear victory for non-violent protest and King was regarded as a highly respected leader in the movement.

Dr. King took part in many marches and demonstrations. A huge civil rights movement in Birmingham, Alabama was followed by major drives for black voter registration. By 1967, Dr. King had been arrested and jailed thirteen times for his non-violent demonstrations.

On August 28, 1963, a massive civil rights demonstration was held in front of the Lincoln Memorial in Washington, D.C. Dr. King spoke to more than 250,000 people about his "dream." This is part of his speech:

> "I have a dream that one day this nation will rise up and live out the true meaning of its creed: 'We hold these truths to be self-evident, that all men are cre-ated equal.'"

> "I have a dream that one day on the red hills of Georgia the sons of former slaves and the sons of former slave owners will be able to sit down together at the table of brotherhood. I have a dream that one day even the state of Mississippi, a state sweltering with the people's injustice, sweltering with the heat of oppres-sion, will be transformed into an oasis of freedom and justice."

> "I have a dream that my four little children will one day live in a nation where they will not be judged by the color of their skin but by the content of their character...."

Dr. Martin Luther King

President Kennedy presented the Civil Rights Bill to Congress in 1963. With the passage of this bill, black Americans at last had a foothold on the road to true freedom.

In 1964, when he was only 35 years old, Dr. King was awarded the Nobel Peace Prize. He was the youngest person to ever win this honor.

On April 4, 1968, Dr. Martin Luther King, Jr. was tragically killed by a sniper in Memphis, Tennessee. The news of his death shocked the world. More than 100,000 people attended his funeral in Atlanta and in the years to come his birthday has been observed as a holiday in most states.

Find the meaning of these vocabulary words in your dictionary.

EQUALITY _____

_____

CIVIL RIGHTS _____

_____

BOYCOTT _____

_____

DEMONSTRATION _____

_____

JUSTICE _____

_____

I have a dream....

Dr. Martin Luther King, Jr.

I Have a Dream Pledge

Martin Luther King had a dream that all men and women, boys and girls, could live together in peace and harmony. He asked that we not judge one another by the color of our skin but rather the content of our character. He also encouraged all people to solve their problems peaceably.

Discuss Martin Luther King's dream with your students. Tell them that they can help to make Dr. King's dream a reality at school and at home. Ask them to make a pledge to not judge other students unfairly and to work harder at finding peaceful means to solve problems in the classroom and on the playground.

Award this badge to children who promise to work for peaceful solutions and brotherhood.

January 15th

Martin Luther King Day

I have a dream...

Ask older children to bring in newspaper and magazine articles about people in the world that are not free. Have them locate information about apartheid in South Africa and persecution in communist countries.

They might like to research people that have demonstrated great courage and risked their lives for freedom and justice, such as, Abraham Lincoln. Harriet Tubman, Mohandas Gandhi, Joan of Arc and Reverend Tutu.

I HAVE A DREAM PLEDGE

**I promise to work harder
at finding peaceful solutions
to problems at home
and at school.**

**I also promise to not judge
other people unfairly
and to help in making
Dr. King's dream a reality.**

_____   _____
signed   date

"Dream" Mobile

Each student can make his own "I HAVE A DREAM...MOBILE" using these simple patterns. Cut the mobile from white construction paper and assemble with thread, as shown.

Read Martin Luther King's story to your class and ask the students to reflect on the "dream" that Dr. King had for our country. Ask each student to write his own "dream for his community, country and world on the appropriate mobile pieces.

Tell them that their "dream" must be one that can succeed only if people care for one another and work together in harmony. Examples might include: world hunger, war, poverty, a clean environment, etc.

for my community!

name

I have a dream...

for my country!

for the world!

Brotherhood

Write your own thoughts about brotherhood using the letters B-R-O-T-H-E-R-H-O-O-D.

B _____

R _____

O _____

T _____

H _____

E _____

R _____

H _____

O _____

O _____

D _____

Eskimos

- THE ESKIMO PEOPLE

- ESKIMO WORD FIND

- SCRIMSHAW AND SNOWGLASSES

- WALRUS PUPPET

- ESKIMO STORY CHARACTERS

- ESKIMO CHILDREN

- CREATIVE WRITING

The Eskimo People

For thousands of years, small groups of people have lived in the cold northern areas of Alaska, Canada, Greenland and Siberia. These are the only
people who have been successful in finding food, clothing and shelter in
these frozen lands.

The "Inuit" people, or Eskimos, of Alaska and Canada are the most well known.
The word "Inuit" means "real people." The word "Eskimo" is an Indian word
for "eaters of raw meat."

Winters are severely cold in these northern regions. The temperature often
stays 25° below zero for weeks at a time. Yet the Eskimos are able to build
homes and find food which allows them to live in this harsh climate.

Summer in the Artic circle is much warmer, but very short. When the snow
melts, the "tundra" is exposed to allow some plants and grasses to grow.

Eskimos do not live in igloos made of snow, as most people think. Ice
houses are built only as temporary shelters during hunting trips in the
winter. The "Igloo" is made of blocks of snow which are carefully cut and
formed into a small round house with a hole in the top for a chimney.

Permanent homes are usually built of wood and whalebone and covered with
seal skins and earth. Family members sleep on raised platforms in one large
room. Seal oil is burned for warmth, as well as light.

The clothing used in these harsh climates is very warm. The Eskimo people
must protect themselves from the severe cold with parkas, boots and mittens
made from fur and hides. Snow goggles are used to protect their eyes from
the glaring snow.

Finding food has always been a struggle for the Eskimos. Sometimes, they
patiently wait for hours in the cold to capture a walrus, seal or polar
bear. Eskimos kill animals only for food or other useful products like oil,
hides, and fur. In the summer, they catch fish, rabbits and sometimes wild
reindeer.

Eskimos use snowshoes to travel short distances on land. Long distant travel is done with dog sleds. Huskies are the only domesticated animals the
Eskimos have known. The dogs are carefully trained to work as a team to
pull the sleds long distances.

Two different types of boats are used to travel by water. The "kayak" is a
one-man canoe which is extremely light and waterproof. It is made of driftwood and sealskin that fits tightly around the waist of the man inside. If
the boat over turns, he will stay dry. The "umiak" is a large boat in which
the entire family can travel. It is made of driftwood, whalebone and walrus
skin.

Eskimos are very warm and gentle people. Families live together in peaceful
harmony while outsiders are made to feel welcome. Little has changed in
their lives in modern times. They understand that each person depends on
the others for his or her survival in the cold, harsh world.

JANUARY

Eskimo Word Find

FIND THESE ESKIMO WORDS IN THE PUZZLE BELOW: ESKIMO, INUIT, IGLOO, SEAL, WALRUS, POLAR BEAR, PARKA, HUSKIES, KAYAK, UMIAK, ALASKA, CANADA, TUNDRA.

ACTIVITY 5

```
A C F T G B V C T U N D R A D C V R Y U J
P F G H Y T D F T G H N J L X C F G H B N
O K M J N I G L O O S D F A E F T G H J J
L D R F G H J K I L R F G S F P A R K A K
A F V G Y B H U J K I L O K C V B H N J A
R D V G B H N M J K L C F A G B C F T G Y
B E A X F T W A L R U S C F T G B H U J A
E C V B N M J K L O P M J N H B G V F R K
A D C G Y U I K L O P M B G C A N A D A T
R S C V G B H N J U M I A K P M N H J Y E
E S K I M O S E R C T V B H N J M K L G F
A E V G S S F T G H J H U S K I E S F T H
Q A C Z S E W D F D V B N M K L P O I Y T
A L H J S D F V B N I N U I T D R G B F D
```

Using six of the words in the puzzle, write a paragraph about what you have learned about the Eskimo people.

_____

_____

_____

_____

_____

_____

_____

_____

JANUARY

Scrimshaw and Snow Glasses

Scrimshaw Medallions

The Eskimo people have always enjoyed the fine art of carving. Ivory from whales and walruses was carved into useful and decorative crafts. During the 18th century, the Eskimos taught carving and scrimshaw skills to many European sailors. These sailors made beautiful belt buckles and jewelry to take back home to their loved ones.

Making scrimshaw medallions in the classroom can be quite easy and a lot of fun!

Mix about 1 cup of plaster of paris to every 2/3 cup of water. Quickly drop spoonfuls of the plaster onto sheets of wax paper. Use a nail or drinking straw to make a hole before it dries.

After it has dried overnight, let the children scratch designs in the plaster using a nail or paper clip. When the design is complete, rub colored chalk over the design and blow away the dust. A clear plastic spray can be applied, if you like. Thread a leather or yarn string through the hole and wear with pride!

Eskimo Snow Glasses

The Inuit people, or Eskimos, made snow glasses that protected their eyes from the reflected glare of the snow. Your students can make snow glasses, too, with just a few simple materials.

Cut strips of poster board or laminated construction paper, measuring about 3" X 16". Cut out as the pattern indicates. Children can color or paint their own creative designs on the glasses.

Children will love wearing their "snow glasses" whether it be in the winter or the sunny summer.

cut

fold

Cut out eye slots with an art knife.

Walrus Puppet

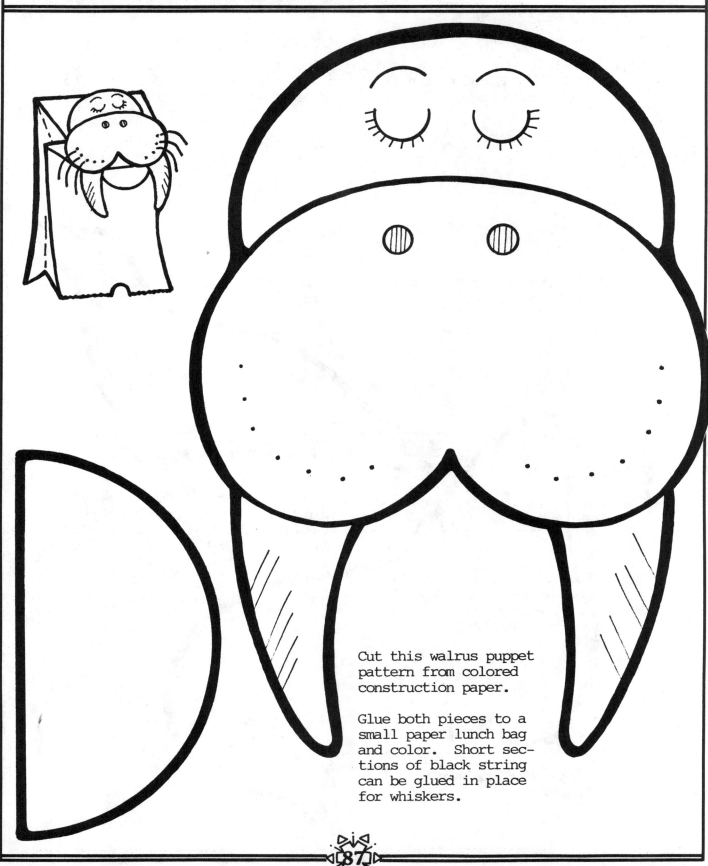

Cut this walrus puppet
pattern from colored
construction paper.

Glue both pieces to a
small paper lunch bag
and color. Short sec-
tions of black string
can be glued in place
for whiskers.

JANUARY

Eskimo Story Characters

These cute characters can be used in flannel board stories about Eskimo life. Cut out and color each illustration. Glue a square of flannel to the back of the picture and apply to the board as you tell the story of the Inuit people.

Enlarged, these characters can be used in a bulletin board display. It's a great way to reinforce various Eskimo words and customs.

Seals provide the Eskimos with much of their food and skins for their clothing.

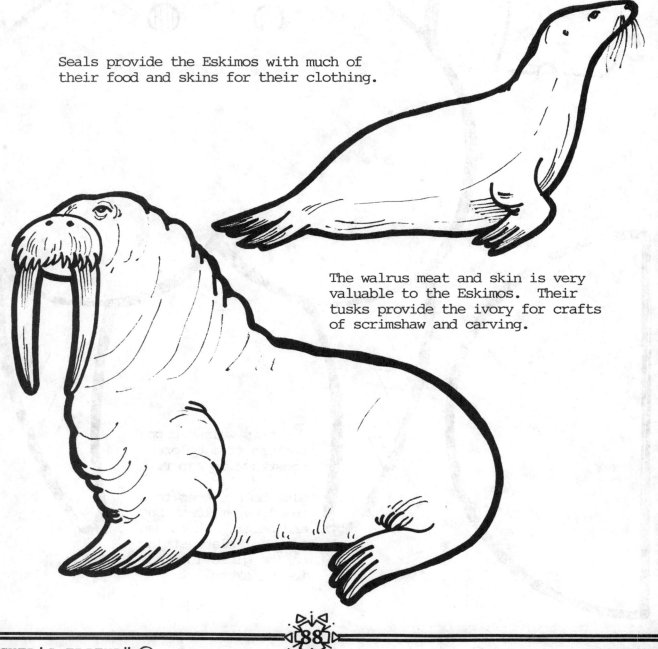

The walrus meat and skin is very valuable to the Eskimos. Their tusks provide the ivory for crafts of scrimshaw and carving.

The Eskimos are very warm and gentle people.

Common names for Eskimo children are Ootah, Nathlook, Inatuk, and Akoik.

Eskimos wear fur jackets called "parkas."

Polar bears provide food for the Eskimo family. Their fur is used to make the warm clothing needed in the winter.

"Mukluks" help keep their feet warm in the cold winters.

A "kayak" is a small one-man boat
made of driftwood and seal skin.
It is extremely light and waterproof.

"Igloos" are temporary
homes made of blocks of
snow. The Eskimo men
build igloos when they
are on long hunting trips.

Sleds pulled by "huskies" are
used to travel great distances
across the snow.

Eskimo Children

Eskimo
Children

JANUARY

Creative Writing

_____

_____

_____

_____

_____

_____

_____

_____

_____

_____

_____

_____

_____

_____

_____

_____

_____

_____

_____

_____

_____

_____

_____

_____

JANUARY

WHAT A GREAT YEAR!

Enlarge a world globe on the class bulletin board. Display the year across the top of the board.

Students can collect articles from newspapers and magazines of events that have taken place during the year. Display the articles around the board.

SNOWMEN AWARDS

Students will love collecting different pattern pieces to complete their snowmen. Award one snowman part for each assignment completed during the week. The last award should be the snowman's top hat. Display the snowmen on the class bulletin board as a motivating winter theme.

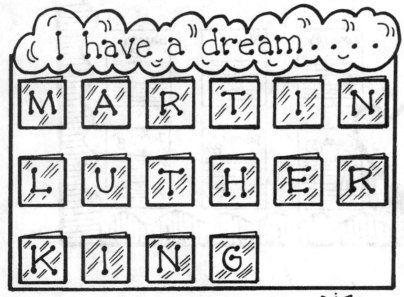

I HAVE A DREAM.....

Ask each student to write a one page report about Martin Luther King. Display the reports in construction paper folders spelling out his name.

Label the top of the board "I have a dream..." and your bulletin board is complete.

and more...

RAINBOW RACES

Brighten up a winter class-room with a colorful rainbow bulletin board. Students cut their own snowflakes that compete to reach the pot of gold. Each snowflake moves ahead as library books are read or multiplication facts learned.

Next month, change the snow-flakes to paper hearts and then to shamrocks in March.

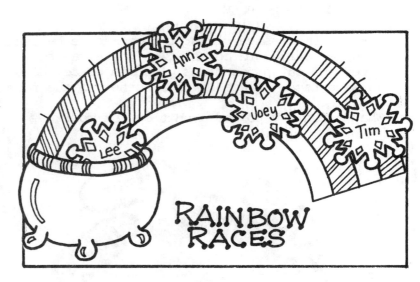

SHORT "I" IGLOO

Ask children to write short "i" words on strips of paper and dis-play them on the class board around a giant paper igloo. As words are collected, write the students' names on the blocks of ice.

The same igloo can be used to display Eskimo reports or winter poems.

COMING SOON!

Look ahead to the new year by listing the highlights of the months to come.

Keep interest high by frequent-ly changing the events.

and more...

CLASSROOM TOTEM POLE

Make an impressive classroom totem pole by asking students to bring in assorted cardboard boxes. The boxes can be covered with construction paper and cut-paper faces glued in place. Assemble the totem pole with masking tape. Place it in a corner of the room for added stability.

What a fun way to end a unit on Eskimos!

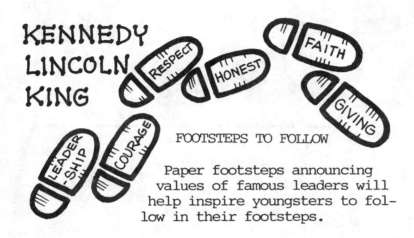

FOOTSTEPS TO FOLLOW

Paper footsteps announcing values of famous leaders will help inspire youngsters to follow in their footsteps.

SIMPLE MONITOR DISPLAY

Cut colored paper plates in half. Write each student's name on one plate half and a classroom job on the remaining half. Match the two halves together and pin them to the class board. Change the classroom duties often, to give everyone a chance.

World Globe

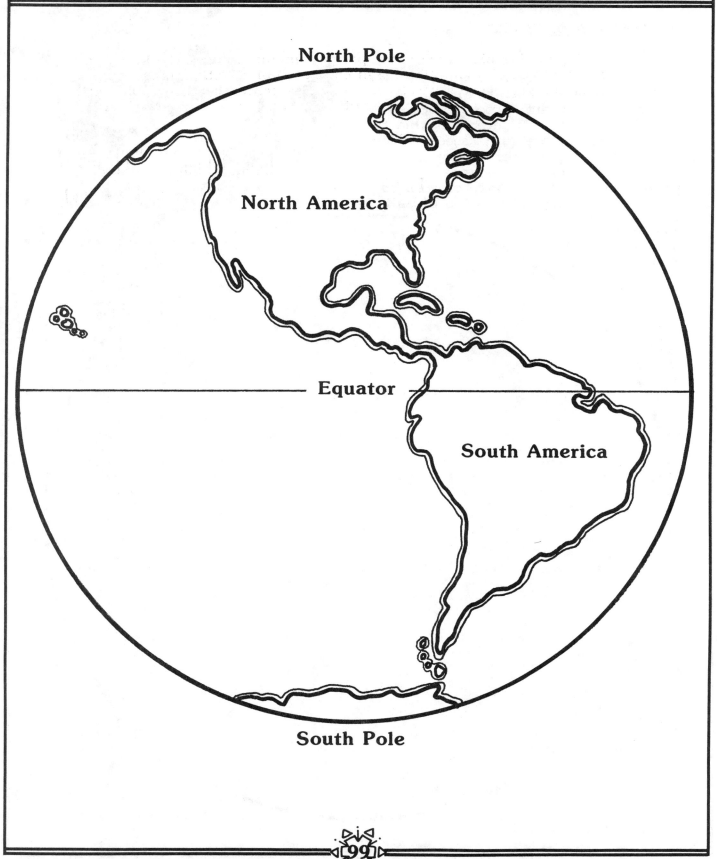

North Pole

North America

Equator

South America

South Pole

JANUARY

Snowman Pattern

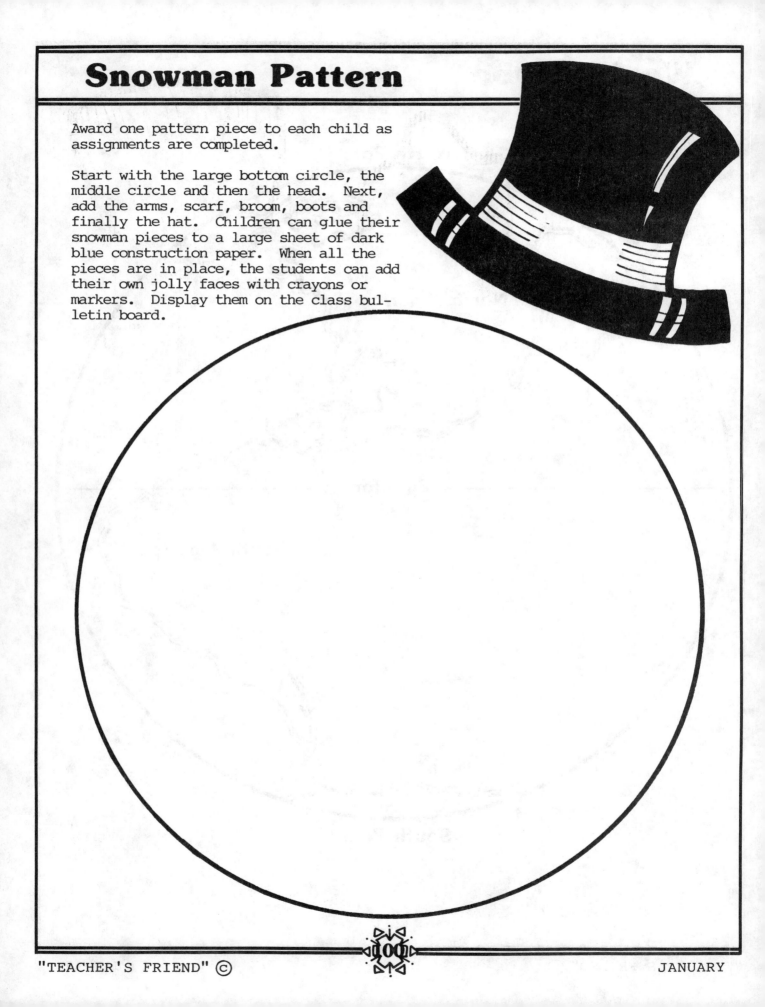

Award one pattern piece to each child as
assignments are completed.

Start with the large bottom circle, the
middle circle and then the head. Next,
add the arms, scarf, broom, boots and
finally the hat. Children can glue their
snowman pieces to a large sheet of dark
blue construction paper. When all the
pieces are in place, the students can add
their own jolly faces with crayons or
markers. Display them on the class bulletin board.

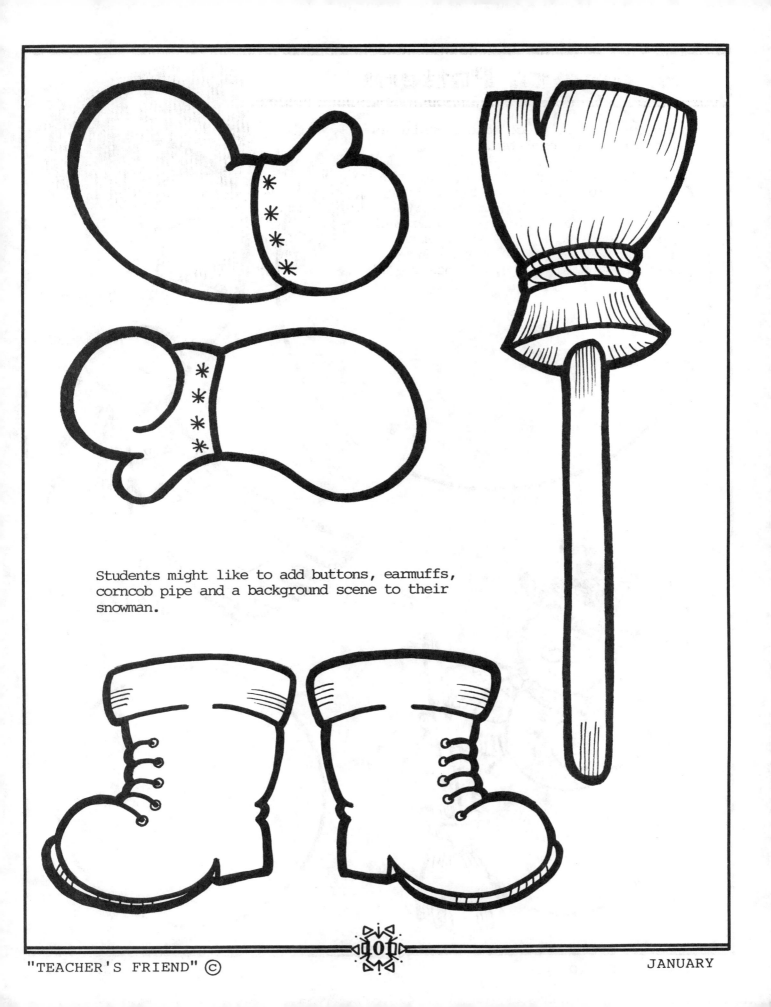

Students might like to add buttons, earmuffs, corncob pipe and a background scene to their snowman.

Snowman Mobile

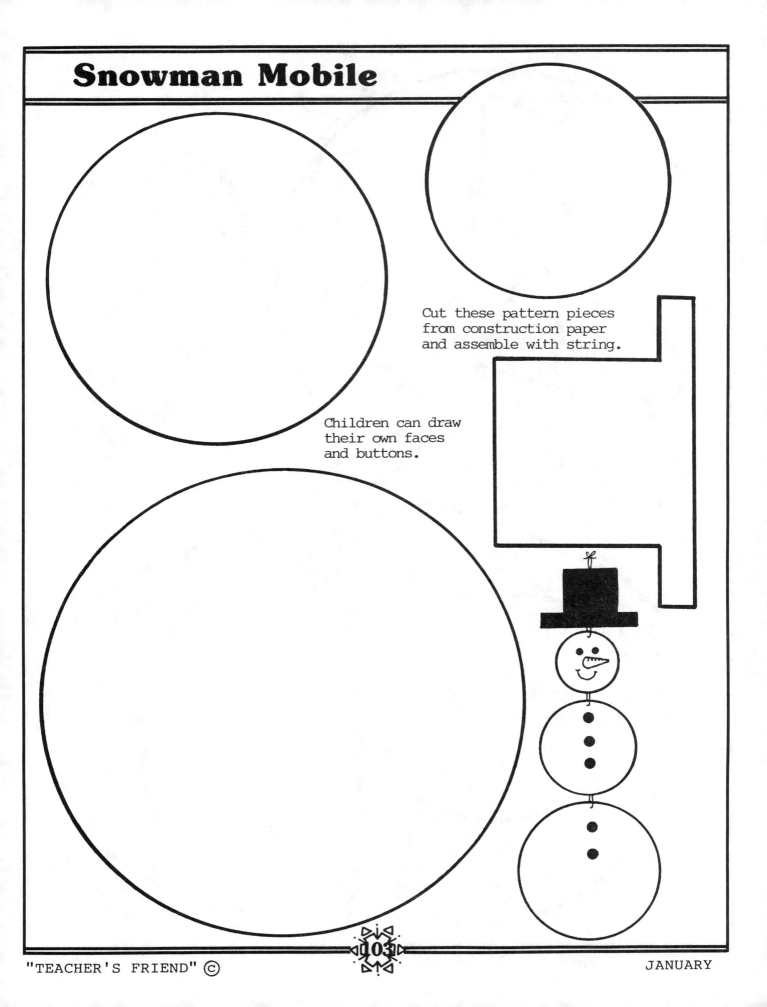

Cut these pattern pieces
from construction paper
and assemble with string.

Children can draw
their own faces
and buttons.

JANUARY

JANUARY

Notes

Answer Key

FIND THESE WINTER WORDS
IN THE PUZZLE: SNOW, ICE,
MITTENS, WINTER, FROST,
COLD, JACKET, SLED, ICICLE,
SNOWFLAKE, SKI, SNOWMAN.

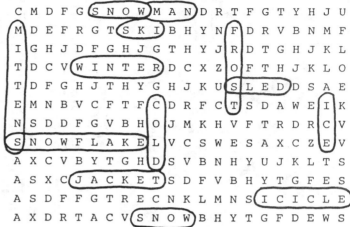

```
C M D F G S N O W M A N D R T F G T Y H J U
M D E F R G T S K I B H Y N F D R V B N M F
I G H J D F G H J G T H Y J R D T G H J K L
T D C V W I N T E R D C X Z O F T H J K L O
T D F G H J T H Y G H J K U S L E D D S A E
E M N B V C F T F C D R F C T S D A W E I K
N S D D F G V B H O J M K H V F T R D R C V
S N O W F L A K E L V C S W E S A X C Z E V
A X C V B Y T G H D S V B N H Y U J K L T S
A S X C J A C K E T S D F V B H Y T G F E S
A S D F F G T R E C N K L M N S I C I C L E
A X D R T A C V S N O W B H Y T G F D E W S
```

FIND THESE NEW YEAR WORDS IN THE PUZZLE BELOW: JANUARY, NEW YEAR, BELLS,
CELEBRATE, MIDNIGHT, FATHER TIME, RESOLUTION, CONFETTI, BALLOONS, CUSTOM,
FRIENDS.

```
G N M K L O P L K M J N H G A S W E R T X
A S W D V F R T F V G E S E D F T G H Y U
F R I E N D S X D R T W U I C F T G B N B
Q E S D F R G T G H N Y F R C U S T O M N
A S E R C V B N H Y T E W S C V F R G D J
A O C V B C O N D V F A F R B D E R T Y Y
X L C O N F E T T I D R S E E C V B N M I
Q U X C V B G F D E B A E F L A S D E R U
A T D F G H X E R T Y H C E L E B R A T E
Z I X C V G T F R E D F G T S D V B N M U
A O F B N M J K F A T H E R T I M E X C T
W N S D B A L L O O N S C D R E T G H Y N
M I D N I G H T V D E R T F G R D S W E R
A S D E W Q X C V J A N U A R Y N H J K L
```

ACTIVITY 2

Answer Key

ACTIVITY 3

```
A M S D F R E T G D C Q A S E D F R G B N M C D S J
A X C M A R C H A C F V B G H N J U N E O U K I G A
A S S D E F R T G J S D E R T G B N H J U K I L I N
P S D S E P T E M B E R F G H Y J U K I O L G T D U
R D F G T H Y J U D F R T G H Y N J U G C H Y U G A
I S W E D C V G T D E C E M B E R D R F T S W A W R
L S X C V B G F D S A W E R T G Y A D E O F R S E Y
X S A F R E T Y H G T R E D C F G T R A B R G H J S
G J U L Y A X M Z S E R C V G T H Y A R E F G V B N
X Z C V B G T A N O V E M B E R K L E R A S E D F
A W S D F R C Y A S D C V F G D C V F G A U G U S T
A S X F E B R U A R Y C V B H J K L O P M N G F D S
```

ACTIVITY 4

Now, unsramble the months.

BDREECEM	December
TUUSGA	August
CMRAH	March
TEROOCB	October
RYUABRFE	February
NEUJ	June
RLPAI	April
VMEONREB	November
AMY	May
UYNJAAR	January
PMEESRBET	September
LJYU	July

```
A C F T G B V C T U N D R A D C V R Y U J
P F G H Y T D F T G H N J L X C F G H B N
O K M J N I G L O O S D F A E F T G H J J
L D R F G H J K I L R F G S F P A R K A K
A F V G Y B H U J K I L O K C V B H N J A
R D V G B H N M J K L C F A G B C F T G Y
B E A X F T W A L R U S C F T G B H U J A
E C V B N M J K L O P M J N H B G V F R K
A D C G Y U I K L O P M B G C A N A D A T
R S C V G B H N J U M I A K P M N H J Y E
E S K I M O S E R C T V B H N J M K L G F
A E V G S S F T G H J H U S K I E S F T H
Q A C Z S E W D F D V B N M K L P O I Y T
A L H J S D F V B N I N U I T D R G B F D
```

ACTIVITY 5

"TEACHER'S FRIEND" ©   12   JANUARY